Young
Lady

YOUNG LADY

Illustration and book design by Donna Stackhouse
https://www.dstackillustration.com

Publishing Services by Telemachus Press, LLC
7652 Sawmill Road
Suite 304
Dublin, Ohio 43016 http://www.telemachuspress.com

Contct the author:
Stacycodesigns.com
www.facebook.com/Elissa.Stacy.3

ISBN: 978-1-956867-39-8 (eBook)
ISBN: 978-1-956867-40-4 (Paperback)

Version 2022.08.03

Young Lady

by

Elissa Stacy

Young Lady,
you don't know how
important you are.

But your worth outweighs the sun.

But your journey
is second to none.

You're here for a reason
so don't second guess.

But remember your mission, it's bigger than the rest...

So stay in your lane
because that's where
the truth lies...

Be honest with yourself, and patient with time.

You're a butterfly for sure, I can see you tryin.

But Young Lady
you're a baby, you're
not ready for flyin...

www.ingramcontent.com/pod-product-compliance
Lightning Source LLC
Chambersburg PA
CBHW041613120626
46551CB00002B/433